ez2 FENG SHUI

A SIMPLE GUIDE TO DECORATING YOUR HOME WITH INTENTION

ez2 FENG SHUI

A SIMPLE GUIDE TO DECORATING YOUR HOME WITH INTENTION

JOY HODGE & SANDY SUE RECTOR

Schiffer Publishing Ltd.
4880 Lower Valley Road • Atglen, PA 19310

Other Schiffer Titles You May Like:

The I Ching Oracle Wheel: A Divination System.
Jim Edward Lucier. ISBN: 978-0-7643-4717-7

Inspiring Butterflies: A 27-Day Course of Self Discovery.
Marge Richards and Ginny Zaboronek.
ISBN: 978-0-7643-3969-1

Carry Me Crystals—Chakra Clearing & Oracle Card Deck. Joanie Eisinger, Elizabeth Jarvis & Peter Jarvis.
ISBN: 978-0-7643-5008-5

What's Your Potion?: Liquid Refreshments to Nourish Body, Mind, and Spirit. Morwyn.
ISBN: 978-0-7643-4954-6

Copyright © 2016 by
Joy Hodge & Sandy Sue Rector

Library of Congress Control Number: 2016945275

Published by Schiffer Publishing, Ltd.
4880 Lower Valley Road
Atglen, PA 19310
Phone: (610) 593-1777; Fax: (610) 593-2002
E-mail: Info@schifferbooks.com

Type set in Helvetica Neue LT Pro
ISBN: 978-0-7643-5194-5
Printed in China

All rights reserved. No part of this work may be reproduced or used in any form or by any means—graphic, electronic, or mechanical, including photocopying or information storage and retrieval systems—without written permission from the publisher.
The scanning, uploading, and distribution of this book or any part thereof via the Internet or any other means without the permission of the publisher is illegal andxxxx punishable by law. Please purchase only authorized editions and do not participate in or encourage the electronic piracy of copyrighted materials.

"Schiffer," "Schiffer Publishing, Ltd.," and the "pen and inkwell" are registered trademarks of Schiffer Publishing, Ltd.

For our complete selection of fine books on this and related subjects, please visit our website at www.schifferbooks.com. You may also write for a free catalog.

Schiffer Publishing's titles are available at special discounts for bulk purchases for sales promotions or premiums. Special editions, including personalized covers, corporate imprints, and excerpts, can be created in large quantities for special needs. For more information, contact the publisher.

We are always looking for people to write books on new and related subjects. If you have an idea for a book, please contact us at proposals@schifferbooks.com.

Without the help and support of our friends and family, this guide would not exist. First and foremost, we thank you!

Acknowledgments

Joy: I would like to thank co-author Sandy Sue Rector for helping me learn how to blend my knowledge of furniture and home decor with the energy of Feng Shui. Also for collaborating with me so we can share this beautifully simple system with the world!

I would also like to thank Ashley Furniture Industries, Inc. and New Classic Home Furnishings for helping me discover my passion for furniture and home decor. They have shown me that there is always more to learn, but to remember to keep my professional and personal life in balance.

Sandy Sue: Thank you Joy Hodge for your determination, devotion, passion, and dedication in making this *EZ2 Feng Shui* a reality. I knew spirit wanted me to create a project as important as this one, and you were the person to make it happen. Thank you!

I also give my deepest thanks and appreciation to all the spiritual teachers and masters before me who have so graciously shared their knowledge and wisdom with the world. Your teachings have not only enriched my life, but the lives of millions across space and time.

Finally, I would like to acknowledge my deepest gratitude to the person who introduced me to Feng Shui back in 1998. Without your genuine interest and caring generosity to help me advance my business and my wellbeing through the powerful principles of Feng Shui, none of this would have ever happened: Marlene Sabatina, you changed my life forever.

"When there is harmony in your environment, there is order in the nation. When there is order in the nation, there is peace in the world."

~Chinese Proverb

Contents

Preface 8
Introduction. 9
How to Use These Cards. 12
Helpful Tips 13
Decorating with The Elements 14
Decorating with Animals 15
The Gua Cards 16
   Advice for: Prosperity/Wealth. 17
   Advice for: Reputation/Fame 17
   Advice for: Relationships/Romance 18
   Advice for: Family 18
   Advice for: Health 19
   Advice for Creativity/Children. 19
   Advice for: Knowledge/Self-Improvement 20
   Advice for Career/Life Path. 20
   Advice for Helpful People/Travel 21

Furniture Tips 22
Yin/Yang Room Cards 23
   Advice for: Master Bedroom (Yin Energy) 24
   Advice for: Youth Bedroom (Yin Energy) 24
   Advice for: Bathroom (Yin Energy) 25
   Advice for: Dining Room (Yin Energy). 25
   Advice for: Outisde Front Entry (Yang Energy). . . 26
   Advice for: Garage (Yang Energy). 26
   Advice for: Hallway (Yang Energy) 27
   Advice for Home Office (Yang Energy) 27
   Advice for: Kitchen (Yang Energy) 28
   Advice for: Laundry Room (Yang Energy). 28
   Advice for: Living Room (Yang Energy) 29
   Advice for: Patio (Yang Energy) 29
   Advice for: Staircase (Yang Energy) 30

Conclusion 31

Preface

Feng Shui has been the cornerstone of our lives for many years. Though our paths with Feng Shui are quite different (Joy as marketing specialist in the home furnishings industry and Sandy Sue as a Feng Shui Master), we soon discovered our mutual respect and appreciation for its ability to significantly enhance our lives and the lives of those around us.

We began working together in 2011, and after several highly rewarding projects where Feng Shui was infused into Joy's home and workspace, the idea to collaborate on a Feng Shui guide was born.

Through researching our own questions about Feng Shui, we realized there had to be an easier and better way to bring these valuable lessons into the home and office. Joy is a visual person and when she created the cards, it helped her immensely as she could stretch the bagua and make it bigger, giving her a clearer picture. A couple cards were also easier to carry than a book, as she slipped them into a handbag—she had all her shopping notes there on those two cards. She was able to focus on one area at a time and it allowed her to budget her decor shopping as well. Our inspiration has been to help those looking to lead more fulfilling, well-balanced lives. The synergy of our own inquiries and the answers we discovered became the foundation of the guide you now hold in your hands.

After reading inspirational books like *The Secret* and learning about the Law of Attraction, I understood how essential the EZ2 Feng Shui guide was to improving the energetic flow and balance in life. Surrounding yourself with positive affirmations to feed your soul while the ego isn't looking, is the easiest way to become the person you want to be and live the life you desire. So whether you live and work alone, share your place with your partner, or care for a growing family or business, it is essential that the space is balanced, loving and supportive because our homes are truly where our hearts live.

We are so excited to share this journey of Feng Shui with you!

Welcome to EZ2 Feng Shui!

Introduction

What is Feng Shui? Pronounced "fung shway," it is the art and practice of creating a balance of energy within your living space (typically a home or office). Our aim with Feng Shui is to allow the energy to flow optimally as you set your intentions for good fortune and health to arrive for those inhabiting the space.

The most important tool of Feng Shui that you will use with your *EZ2 Feng Shui* guide is the *Bagua* (pronounced *Ba-gwa*), a map of the energy in your home or room. You'll see there are nine sections, individually known as *Guas*. These Guas are significant because they each represent a specific focus or intention in your life that must be balanced and supported for good energy flow. Look over the areas and identify the Guas that you feel need to be worked on first, as this will give you a place to start.

If finances are an issue, start with the Prosperity/Wealth Gua. If you're lonely and wish to attract a mate, start with the Relationships/Romance Gua. Keep your intentions positive, as if you already have the things you want, not on the LACK of. Be grateful, thankful, and blessed. What you think about, you bring about. If you focus on lack, you will get more of it!

Prosperity/Wealth Gua

Focus on this Gua when you want to increase your wealth and abundance. As you decorate/redecorate, set the intention of how much money you want, unlimited bank accounts, and bills paid off. Focus on financial freedom. The element here is wood, for growth, so think of your money growing.

Reputation/Fame Gua

Focus on this Gua when you want to improve your reputation or gain fame for something. Make sure when working on this area you think positive thoughts about how other people perceive you. Think about what you want—respect, recognition, intelligence, beauty, and talent are all things we desire. Make sure to start your intentions with "I am…" not "I wish I was…" or you will focus on lack. The element for this Gua is fire, which attracts attention.

Relationships/Romance Gua

Work in this Gua when you desire to change or enhance your relationship status. Think about your ideal mate, if you don't already have one, and what they represent to you. Is the person attractive, healthy, wealthy, a good dancer, funny? Has the fire gone out in an existing relationship that you wish to rekindle? Accents of red (fire) add passion. Your intentions here sound something like, "I am so blessed to have the loving relationship that I've always desired." The element for this Gua is earth, which can help you feel grounded and secure.

Family Gua

Focus on this Gua if your family needs harmonizing. The beauty of families are that they are made of people who we may or may not have chosen as friends. There are in-laws and blended families that are so much more supportive when there is harmony. We have more strength when our families love and support each other. "I am so grateful that I have a family that loves and supports me." The element here is wood, for growth.

Health Gua

This Gua is so important, yet many times taken for granted until our health is compromised. Pay special attention to your thoughts, thinking things such as "I'm so blessed to have the gift of good health..." and "my body is strong and healthy." Because this is the center of the Bagua, many times it's the middle of the room or office and there is nothing to decorate. If this is the case, it may be a good place to stand each day and just give thanks and set an intention for good health. The element here is earth to help you feel grounded and secure.

Creativity/Children Gua

The focus of this Gua is to increase your creativity and/or if you are trying to conceive children, look at the energy here. We all have an inner child within us and this is the place to address it. Homemade crafts, art, writing/journaling, and games are perfect to help you relax and break through the "mental block" from your next idea. This card deck is an example of that! The Children Gua reminds us to "lighten up" our attitudes and remember to play. The element of this Gua is metal, for clarity and purity.

Knowledge/ Self-Improvement Gua

This Gua focuses on your education and learning. Not just school or college, but also spiritually, if you choose. As we go through life, we are never done learning. Education keeps us interested and interesting. As adults, we get to choose the subjects that are important to us and our life's purpose. This is a great place to store your *EZ2 Feng Shui* card deck! "I am so thankful for the knowledge and wisdom that I have received, as well as for the teachers that have put their energy into teaching me." The element here is earth, which grounds us.

Career/Life Path Gua

Focus on this Gua if you are wanting to change or enhance your career or life path. A good intention is "I am so grateful for my career and I appreciate how I am respected." Or "My career is very rewarding and I look forward to the new advancements to come." The element for this Gua is water, which represents flexibility, strength, flow of money, and new beginnings.

Helpful People/Travel Gua

If your life needs more friends and an increase in travel, focus here. This Gua helps you to attract all types of friends, physical and spiritual. Focus on where you want to travel, what to see and do. Travel is good for the soul! Set the intention, "I am so blessed that I have been able to travel to ___ and I look forward to when I am going to ___." Or "I am so thankful that I have so many friends that love and help me." The element for this Gua is metal for clarity and purity.

Each of the Room cards in the card deck are labeled "Yin" or "Yang." Yin and Yang represent two perceived opposites that are actually complementary to one another. Yin energy is soft, relaxing, and spa-like where you should keep energy low and colors muted. Yang has high energy with a lot of movement and fun, bright colors.

Rather than simply furnishing and decorating, the power of Feng Shui comes when you positively set the intention to improve your life and the lives of those you care about most: your family, friends, and colleagues. There is a saying, "Birds of a feather, flock together." It simply means if you are kind, loving, and generous, you will attract others who are kind, loving, and generous. This easy-to-use card deck is meant to be your personal guide as you furnish and decorate your space with the optimal pieces, colors, and placement that will enhance and balance the flow of energy.

How to Use These Cards

- Lay the Gua cards in exactly the order they appear on the Bagua Map.

- Lay the Room cards, according to your floor plan, on top of the Gua cards, starting with your front entrance along the bottom. Your front door (entry) should be in either Knowledge/Self-Improvement, Career/Life Path, or Helpful People/Travel Guas. Feel free to use the card as a guide and to stretch out the Gua cards if you need more room.

- Think about the troubles or challenges in your life and select the Gua and Room that must be addressed first. Follow the tips on the Room and Gua cards. If one card conflicts with the other (i.e., one card says to use water decor and the other one says not to use water decor), follow the advice on the Room card.

- If, after laying out all of your Room cards you find that you have a Gua without a Room card on top of it, it is considered a "missing gua." This can be remedied by focusing on that Gua in each separate room.

Helpful Tips

- **REMOVE ALL CLUTTER.** Nothing slows good energy faster than a lot of "stuff." If you haven't used it or worn it in the last year, sell or donate it. If it has emotional value, take a picture of it and/or find a safe place to store it. Do this one Gua at a time and it won't feel so overwhelming. LESS IS BEST.

- Throw out anything that's broken, chipped, damaged, or stained. This includes dishes, bedding, towels, pictures, plastic food containers, and expired food.

- After you've completed each Gua in the house, go back and Feng Shui each room, remembering to put the bottom of the Bagua Map at the entrance to the room. This way, all rooms will have balance. Each room should have predominant features pertaining to its Gua, but should still involve all the elements in the appropriate places. Use pictures of butterflies and/or dragonflies in any Gua that needs transformation.

Decorating with the Elements

WOOD		Furniture, plants (live OR silk).
	Color	Green.
FIRE		Lights, candles, electronics, leather, animal prints, pictures of people.
	Color	Red
EARTH		Pottery, ceramics, granite, tile, slate, travertine, concrete, stone, brick.
	Color	Beige/earth tones, yellow.
METAL		Iron, gold, bronze, silver, copper, brass.
	Color	White, gold, bronze, silver, grey.
WATER		Aquarium, fountain, mirror (whole, not fragmented), glass.
	Color	Black.

Decorating with Animals

Nature provides us with so much inspiration and support through the animal kingdom. Animals belong to the fire element, but each gua needs a little fire for balance. Think about the animal and what it means to you. Think about its strengths and what the animal is known for. For example, an elephant is known for its strength, memory, and longevity; therefore, I would like it in my health and/or career gua.

Prosperity/Wealth: Animals used to create income and/or abundance and wealth. Farm animals, fish, and also the bull, as it pertains to a optimistic stock market. Lobster and crab are usually the most expensive items on a restaurant menu.

Reputation/Fame: How do you want others to see you? Horse has strength and beauty, dogs are loyal. Chinese believe a rooster protects your reputation if placed in your career gua or office.

Relationships/Romance: Pair of cranes, lovebirds. Think about animals that mate for life.

Family: Ducks, quail, animals shown in family form. Mama bear is known for protecting her cubs.

Health: Tortoise, elephant, macaw, and koi are all known for longevity.

Creativity/Children: Many household pets are treated like our children. Dogs, cats, and domestic animals are great in this gua, as well as the "happy, laughing" animals like coyote and dolphin.

Knowledge/Self-Improvement: Owls, elephants, and monkeys are known for their intelligence.

Career/Life Path: Bee, horse, elephant, eagle, fish, and also "King of the Jungle" lion are good ideas.

Helpful People/Travel: Think animals that migrate (travel) as they do so in large groups (helpful people).

The Gua Cards

ADVICE FOR:
Prosperity/Wealth

Colors: Purple, dark blue, green
Shape: Rectangle
Element: Wood

Symbols of luxury, money, coins.
Water fountain and/or pictures of flowing water.
Fish aquarium, pictures of fish, or mobile.
Plants with rounded leaves (live or silk).
Photos of desired possessions/expensive items.
Striped fabrics or wallpaper.

ADVICE FOR:
Reputation/Fame

Colors: Red, orange, green
Shape: Triangle
Element: Fire

Candles, lights, and electrical items.
Pictures of people and/or animals.
Animal print fabrics or leather.
Sunrise or image of the sun.
Trophies, accomplishments, and awards.
Chairs with high backs.

ADVICE FOR: Relationships/Romance

Colors: Pink, red, beige
Shape: Square
Element: Earth

Things in pairs (i.e., sofa with two cushions; pillows in pairs).
Low, heavy furniture that hugs the ground.
Pair of swans, cranes, ducks, doves, geese, lovebirds.
Picture or statue of a romantic couple.
Hearts.
Pair of candles.

ADVICE FOR: Family

Colors: Green, brown, blue
Shape: Rectangle
Element: Wood

Tall wood items like armoire, chest, or bookshelf.
Live or silk tree.
Vertical striped fabric or wallpaper.
Plants—bamboo, jade, philodendron, peace lily.
Quail, partridge, ducks in family form.
Family photos in wood frame.

ADVICE FOR:
Health

ADVICE FOR:
Creativity/Children

Colors: Yellow, beige, red
Shape: Square
Element: Earth

Colors: White, grey, pastels
Shape: Circle or Oval
Element: Metal

Affirmations for peace, love, joy.
Healthy plant (live or silk).
Yellow flowers (live, silk, or picture).
Candles.
Salt lamp.
Artwork that symbolizes health or a healthy person.

Whimsical, fun.
Uplifting and playful.
Colorful.
Artwork.
Toys, games, music.
Crafts/hobbies.

ADVICE FOR:
Knowledge/Self-Improvement

Colors: Blue, beige, black
Shape: Square
Element: Earth

Heavy, grounding furniture.
Mountain picture.
Spiritual/religious symbols.
Books on self-improvement.
Affirmations and/or intentions.
Wisdom symbols, like owls/angels.

ADVICE FOR:
Career/Life Path

Colors: Black, grey, dark blue
Shape: Wavy
Element: Water

Mirror (not reflecting the door).
Glass table(s).
Art with water flowing AWAY from door.
Moving objects—clock, reclining furniture.
Aquarium or fountain.

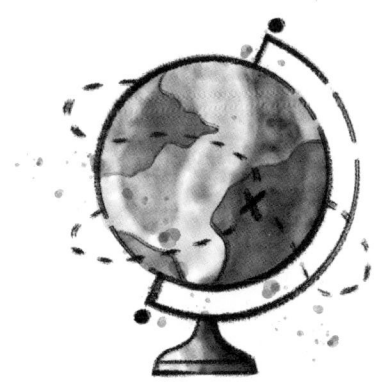

ADVICE FOR:
Helpful People/Travel

Colors: Grey, white, metallics
Shape: Circle
Element: Metal

Travel Photos.
Artwork of groups of people.
Spiritual/religious symbols.
Store luggage here, if possible.
Flowers in all colors.
Rabbits, because they multiply!
Maps/globe.

Furniture Tips

Bedroom: Two nightstands, each with a lamp, unless a child's room, then only one. Headboard should be solid, not metal, and against a solid wall, not under a window or next to the door, if possible. NO MIRRORS. Replace mirror with a romantic piece of wall art. Mattress should be in good condition and comfortable. Do not use under bed for storage.

Dining Room: Round, oval, or rectangle table with rounded corners. Mirror reflecting table doubles the amount of food and increases abundance. Even number of chairs.

Living Room: Use Gua card guidelines, but make sure all seating is comfortable and in good condition. Reclining furniture is good energy for this room.

Home Office: Use Gua card guidelines, but make sure there is enough storage to keep clutter at bay. For example, a bookshelf with doors.

Patio: Use Gua card guidelines along with recommended furniture type for your geographical location. Must be comfortable and in good condition.

Yin/Yang Room Cards

Master Bedroom
Yin Energy

- Earth Tones.
- Sensual, romantic images that relax and inspire you.
- Only photos of the people who sleep in this room.
- Everything in pairs—pillows, candles, etc.
- No water or pictures of water scenes.
- No computers or exercise equipment.
- Add passion with accents of red and/or pink.
- No LIVE plants; use silk.
- Statue to bring stability and protection— spiritual/religious symbol.

Youth Bedroom
Yin Energy

- Use artwork THEY have created and hang at THEIR eye level.
- Display their trophies and accomplishments at their eye level.
- Pastel colors to calm the energy.
- Pictures of family and friends for security.
- CALM images for better sleep.
- Avoid bunk beds. Use a trundle bed if necessary.
- Desk facing the door or on same wall as the door.
- Something to symbolize what they want to be when they grow up.
- Night light.

Bathroom
Yin Energy

- Small plant (live or silk) on top of toilet tank.
- No photos of family or friends.
- Nature pictures.
- Add candles, incense, or fragrance.
- Keep toilet lid closed.
- Keep it FRESH: fluffy towels, matching rug.
- Earth tones.

Dining Room
Yin Energy

- Use tablecloth or placemats.
- Plants and flowers.
- Earthy colors, also red.
- Landscape pictures.
- Lighting on a dimmer switch/candles.
- Should be a reflection of who you are.
- Avoid blues/blacks.
- Big mirror reflecting the table.

Outside Front Entry
Yang Energy

- Solid black welcome mat.
- Potted red flowers on either side of front door.
- "Welcome" sign.
- Metal wind chime.
- Statue to bring stability/protection.
- Well lit.

Garage
Yang Energy

- Organize and clear clutter.
- Store chemicals safely.
- Store all items in cabinets, if possible or use attractive storage bins.
- Hang pictures and posters—make it a fun place!
- Organize tools, sharp objects out of sight.
- Make sure doors open/close smoothly.
- "Welcome" or "Welcome Home" sign.

Hallway
Yang Energy

- Runner rug, if bare floor.
- Landscape artwork.
- Upward lighting.
- Use light-colored paint.

Home Office
Yang Energy

- Live plants.
- Desk facing doorway, or hang small mirror to see behind you.
- Flowers.
- Certificates, diplomas, pictures, mottos, and images that symbolize what you want to accomplish.
- Law of Attraction—write down goals and intentions and store them here.
- Keep phone on the right side of your desk.

Kitchen
Yang Energy

- Bright colors.
- Stove = Abundance. Use ALL burners.
- Fresh flowers, bowl of fruit.
- Discard damaged items: dented cans, chipped plates, stained plasticware.
- No photos of friends/family.
- No knives on the counter. Store them in a cupboard or drawer out of sight.
- Pictures of fruits/vegetables.
- Plants/herbs on top of refrigerator and next to sink.

Laundry Room
Yang Energy

- Well lit.
- Fun artwork.
- Attractive storage bins. No clutter.
- Keep washing machine and dryer closed.
- No leaky hoses.
- Keep laundry room door closed.
- Put clean clothes away immediately.
- Use environmentally friendly detergents.
- Plant and/or flowers.

Living Room
Yang Energy

- Family photos.
- Plants and flowers.
- Landscape of sunrise, water, or mountains.
- Inspirational people.
- Reclining furniture.

Patio
Yang Energy

- Windchime, flags, windsock.
- Lights around perimeter.
- Lots of plants.
- Furniture should be comfortable and in good condition.
- Hummingbird feeder.
- Candles/lanterns.
- Round pot with flowers in colors to reflect specific Gua.

Staircase
Yang Energy

- No water under the stairs.
- Keep it well lit—use uplighting.
- Use plants to slow down the energy.
- Use space under stairs for organized storage.
- Hang attractive and positive wall art with upward movement.
- Keep clear of clutter. Do not leave things on the stairs.

Conclusion

Our hope is that you will feel any heavy energy lift in your home, and these simple changes bring you comfort and happiness. Enjoy making your home a better place to be. Know that you are never really "done" with this project, as you will always find areas that may need adjusting. We acknowledge that every room, home, and office is different, so please understand this guide is simply general information to set you on the right path towards a well-balanced life based on your living space. If you are looking to dive deeper into the essence of Feng Shui and how it can truly enhance your life, we strongly suggest consulting a professional Feng Shui Master.

Each year, pick a room to refresh. It may include a complete remodel, a modest refurnish, or depending on your budget, just some new toss pillows and flowers. Whatever you choose, LOVE your home. Make it a place where you can relax and enjoy life. Invite your friends and family over. Get to know your neighbors. Share some good food and conversation. Use the good dishes. Most of all, be thankful for your blessings!